The Chronicles Of Jane, Book Seven

by Alan Haehnel

Single copies of plays are sold for reading purposes only. The copying or duplicating of a play, or any part of play, by hand or by any other process, is an infringement of the copyright. Such infringement will be vigorously prosecuted.

Baker's Plays
7611 Sunset Blvd.
Los Angeles, CA 90042
bakersplays.com

NOTICE

This book is offered for sale at the price quoted only on the understanding that, if any additional copies of the whole or any part are necessary for its production, such additional copies will be purchased. The attention of all purchasers is directed to the following: this work is fully protected under the copyright laws of the United States of America, the British Commonwealth, including Canada, and all other countries of the Copyright Union. Violations of the Copyright Law are punishable by fine or imprisonment, or both. The copying or duplication of this work or any part of this work, by hand or by any process, is an infringement of the copyright and will be vigorously prosecuted.

This play may not be produced by amateurs or professionals for public or private performance without first submitting application for performing rights. Licensing fees are due on all performances whether for charity or gain, or whether admission is charged or not. Since performance of this play without the payment of the licensing fee renders anybody participating liable to severe penalties imposed by the law, anybody acting in this play should be sure, before doing so, that the licensing fee has been paid. Professional rights, reading rights, radio broadcasting, television and all mechanical rights, etc. are strictly reserved. Application for performing rights should be made directly to BAKER'S PLAYS.

No one shall commit or authorize any act or omission by which the copyright of, or the right to copyright, this play may be impaired. No one shall make any changes in this play for the purpose of production.

Publication of this play does not imply availability for performance. Both amateurs and professionals considering a production are strongly advised in their own interest to apply to Baker's Plays for written permission before starting rehearsals, advertising, or booking a theatre.

Whenever the play is produced, the author's name must be carried in all publicity, advertising and programs. Also, the following notice must appear on all printed programs, "Produced by special arrangement with Baker's Plays."

Licensing fees for THE CHRONICLES OF JANE, BOOK SEVEN are based on a per performance rate and payable one week in advance of the production.

Please consult the Baker's Plays website at www.bakersplays.com or our current print catalogue for up to date licensing fee information.

Copyright © 2001 by Alan Haehnel
Made in U.S.A.
All rights reserved.

THE CHRONICLES OF JANE, BOOK SEVEN
ISBN **978-0-87440-136-3**
#1360-B

The Chronicles of Jane, Book Seven was originally produced at Hartford High School, Hartford, VT on February 17th, 2000. It was directed by Alan Haehnel. The cast was as follows:

Jane	Faith Wood
Norman	Josh Abetti
Rhythm Coordinator	Anthony Paino
Mrs. Sniperly	Allison Cameron
Nymphs of Slumber	Bridget Dornik, Jess Poludin Hannah Lowes, Rachel Ladd
Computer	James Lamdin
Stewart	Joe Guarino
Cecelia	Emily Wood
Time	Jacob Sotak
Procrastination	Colin Kennedy
Groupies	Christina Clark, Dan Wyzik Chris Hamilton, Bethany Kent Erin Riley, Molly Brown Kat North, Mike Post Liz Wyzik, Carma Gilcrist Taylor Haynes, Angela Paladino Cassie Fitch, Esther Garcia-Martin Johannah Riling, Katie Sensenich Ingrid Weiss, Maria Paino Sarah Finney, Robin Clavelle Hope Hayes, Julia Eddy

AUTHOR'S NOTE

My aim in writing "The Chronicles of Jane, Book Seven," was to create a vehicle for expressing, in its most vibrant form, adolescent energy. Since I knew I would also be directing "Jane," I wrote with a directorial challenge in mind as well: no set, no props, no mechanical sound effects; just actors, light, and a space. My production of "Jane," in order to fulfill both my writing and directing goals, ended up being a very physical piece. Using a lot of improvisation and calling on student expertise whenever possible, our version of "Jane" had actors marching in formations, chanting and singing, beating out rhythms of the floor and on themselves, and climbing on one another.

I'm telling you this for two reasons: first, I hope you, too, will try to achieve these goals as you produce "Jane" - to make the show an expression of adolescent energy and to create the play without using props, sets or mechanical sound effects.

My second reason for including this note is to justify my intentionally sparse stage directions. The script might have been several pages longer and included diagrams and music if I had wished to detail precisely how I directed "The Chronicles of Jane, Book Seven." However, my wish is that every director and cast who undertakes "Jane" will start as we did: with a concept, with a few words, with a willingness to display as many talents and exciting ideas as a cooperative group can discover. Let no "Jane" look like another.

DEDICATION

To My Niece Maren
Who Died Young While "Jane" Was Being Born.
The Energy of Her Life Inspired Us.

CHARACTERS

JANE
NORMAN
MRS. SNIPERLY
NYMPHS OF SLUMBER
COMPUTER
STEWART
CECELIA
TIME
PROCRASTINATION
GROUPIES A-R
GROUPIES 1-26
JAZZ GROUPIES 1-4

If one were to cast "Jane" with a separate actor for each character in the play (with four Nymphs of Slumber), the cast size would be 59. However, the play lends itself well to doubling and tripling of characters, so the show can successfully be produced using as few as 30 actors. The gender of most of the characters is also flexible.

THE CHRONICLES OF JANE, BOOK SEVEN

(The stage is empty except for an eight foot tall book, downstage right. On its cover, ornately printed: "The Chronicles of Jane." Under dim light, the cast enters from the wings. They walk to center stage and kneel in three tight rows, running upstage to downstage. They raise their hands and begin to hum as the lights come up slowly. Jane rises from upstage of the rows and settles, cross-legged, atop the hands. She seems to float along this humming river of hands; two attendants walk beside her, providing balance. When the cast has passed her to the front of the lines, Jane is lowered so she can stand in front of the rows. She claps her hands once. The humming stops. Jane looks straight out at the audience. She is wearing an orange and yellow tie-dyed sundress; other cast members are also in tie-dye--purple, blue and white shorts, long-sleeved shirts, and knee-pads. After a moment, Jane speaks.)

JANE. I am... *(The hands come down suddenly, thumping like a drum.)* Jane. *(The cast beats twice on the floor.)* One-two-three-four.

(The cast begins to chant "J-J-J-J" in time to the cadence Jane has just established. Using crisp, unison formations, the group makes a "v" with Jane, still downstage center, as the tip. When the formation has been completed, the cast thrusts its hands in the air and shouts "Jane!")

JANE *(cont)*. Do it.

(The "v" collapses back into lines. Jane runs to the back of the group and climbs on the shoulders of several cast members. Standing high, she proclaims herself again.)

JANE *(cont)*. I am...

(She falls forward, landing in the arms of the rest of the cast, hereafter referred to as Groupies.)

GROUPIES *(as she falls)*. Jane! *(As they flip her over to land seated in the arms of her Groupies)* Jaaaane!
JANE. Nice to meet... me.

(The Groupies beat out a cadence on their bodies as they move into a semi circle around Jane. During this next pattered segment, they fill in the space between stanzas with drumming, produced on the floor or on their bodies. Jane dances during these sections, the epitome of confidence.)

JANE *(cont)*. The name is plain, I am aware,
But don't you be mistaken.
I'm sixteen years chock full of nerve
and nowhere near to breaking.

I'm five foot five, a hundred and twelve
Every bit of it solid as steel.
My brain's on fire with sparking thoughts
You better know I'm the real deal.

This stage is mine for the next small bit
And I've got a story to tell,

And if you don't like it, well, listen to this,
Take your ticket straight down to...
    ALL. Jane!
    JANE. Enough of the noise,
Enough of the beat;
You've had the hors d'oeuvres -
Now I'll serve the meat.

> *(Silence. Jane crosses to the book. The stage goes dim except for the light on the book and on Groupie A.)*

    GROUPIE A *(to the audience)*. Ladies and Gentlemen, I ask for your reverence. Jane is about to open one of this century's most important documents - The Chronicles of Jane. Within the covers of this magnificent book one can find tales of horror and delight, evoking every conceivable emotion from the lowest depression to the highest ecstasy. These volumes do not document a world, a nation, nor even a community. No, The Jane Chronicles are by and about one person, one colossal figure on the American landscape: Jane. Consider yourself among the fortunate few in history to witness this moment.

> *(As the Groupies sing a wordless song of awe, Jane opens the "front cover," revealing that the book is actually a box. Jane begins to take out and leaf through several smaller books from inside the box; all are replicas of the large book.)*

    GROUPIE 1. Jane, will we tell them of your first battle with your brother, the Evil Stewart?

JANE. Book Two of the Jane Chronicles, verses five through fifty-five. Stewart eats dust. No. That will not be the story tonight.

GROUPIE 2. What of the great journey to Wal-Mart and the return of the heinous flared pants?

JANE. A worthy tale, a lusty tale, a frightening tale, indeed. But no. That will not be the story tonight.

GROUPIE 3. Oh, Jane, let us tell them of your struggle against the almost-unmentionable, the dark and disgusting, the loathsome Monique.

ALL *(spitting out the word)*. Monique!

JANE. The whole of Book Four of the Jane Chronicles, devoted to my battle with that almost-unmentionable hag. Nay. That will not be the story tonight.

GROUPIE 4. How about...?

JANE. Silence, my minions! I feel the story well up in me like mozzarella boiling on a pizza pie. Tonight - Book Seven of the Chronicles of Jane: The Term Paper.

(A general scream and hush from the group.)

GROUPIE 5. Do you think they can handle it, Jane?

GROUPIE 6. They look a little feeble for that one, don't you think?

GROUPIE 7. I'm not sure I feel quite up to it myself.

JANE. We will begin. We have not come to coddle. We will begin! *(The Groupies begin to move, getting into places to form Jane's room. They freeze when they hear Jane say her next words; some of them try to hide.)* Who will be my stand-in? You?

GROUPIE 8. Ah, Jane, I did it the last time; my ankle is just a little tender.

JANE. You?

GROUPIE 9. My mother really would rather I didn't, Jane. Sorry.

JANE. Who will be my stand-in?

(The group looks around, uncomfortable.)

JANE *(cont)*. Drop down, all of you who are cowards! Drop down, and let those remaining be they who would rise to the lofty standard required of a Jane proxy! Drop down, cowards!

(All drop. Silence for a beat, then Norman enters.)

NORMAN. I'm here, I'm here. I know I'm late, but let me tell you why. See, I was on my way over when this bus crossed right in front of me and, you wouldn't believe it, but a monkey jumped out the window, right onto the front of my car. Seriously. *(Crossing to Jane)* Janey, hi. Listen, I even got that drum stuff down. Look. *(He starts to beat out the cadence, but Jane silences him with a hand on his shoulder.)* What? *(He looks around - everyone is staring at him.)* What?

JANE. Brave and noble soul.

NORMAN. Oh, yeah? *(Jane strips off her dress with a single swipe and hands it to Norman.)* Whoa. What'd you do that for?

JANE. Wear this with pride, noble Norman.

NORMAN. Wear it? *(Dawning realization.)* Oh, no, I'm not doing this. *(The Groupies cheer and gather around Norman, congratulating him. Several quickly pull him offstage, despite his protests. Meanwhile, two Groupies have put a new dress on Jane, identical to the one she just took off.)* Whoa, wait a minute! I'm a guy - this is against the law. You can't do this!

    JANE *(over Norman)*. We will begin! *(The Groupies move, accompanied by a cadence, into position to begin. They form the walls, the desk, the chair, and so on. Throughout the play, the group moves to represent what Jane narrates. They become the sets and the characters suggested by her words.)* Has the scene been readied?

    GROUPIES. Ready!
    JANE. Sound off.
    GROUPIE B. Wall.
    GROUPIE C. Wall.
    GROUPIE D. Wall.
    GROUPIE E. Chair, wooden, sturdy. A couple of screws loose.
    GROUPIE F. Wall.
    GROUPIE G. Wall.
    GROUPIES H AND I *(full of cheerful energy)*. Here she sleeps, here she dreams, here she lays her lovely head. We're just honored, pleased as punch, to be our Janey's comfy bed.
    GROUPIE J. Wall.
    GROUPIE K. Wall.
    GROUPIE L. Wall.
    GROUPIES M AND N *(dull as dirt)*. We are Jane's desk.
    GROUPIE M. We have no cutesy rhyme.
    GROUPIE N. We're just the desk.
    GROUPIE M. You can write on us.
    GROUPIE N. You can stand on us.
    GROUPIES M AND N. We're just the desk.
    TIME. One clock here. I'll say more later.
    GROUPIE O. Wall.
    GROUPIE P. Wall.

GROUPIE Q. I am a 2x4 in the wall, a support beam, thus making me a stud. Grr.

COMPUTER *(This line should be modified to reflect the current technology.)*. One computer. Gateway E-3200 450. Intel Pentium III Processor, 450 MegaHertz with 512 K Cache. 6.8 Gigabytes 5400RPM Ultra Hard Drive, and a fully functionally joy stick. Need I go on? I don't think so.

GROUPIE R. And I am the power cord for the computer. Here is my three-prong adapter where I attach to the floor. I know what you're thinking. You're thinking, big deal, a power cord. Well, let me tell you something. I'm important. I am integral to this production. You'll see! You just wait! You'll see, all of you! I may just lie here most of the time with my prongs stuck in the floor, but you'll see!

ALL REMAINING GROUPIES PLAYING THE WALL. Wall!

> *(Jane starts to read from Book Seven of the Jane Chronicles. Clearly, she knows the text well enough that she can often deliver long passages without reading.)*

JANE. I am in my room. *(She pauses, waiting for Norman's appearance.)* I am in my room! *(Norman is suddenly pushed on stage, wearing the "Jane dress," looking extremely reluctant.)* I am in my room, feeling the weight of my situation chain me to my desk.

NORMAN. Jane? *(He crosses to her, extremely self-conscious.)* I don't want to be your stand-in.

JANE. Norman, do you have any idea what a privilege it is to be me?

NORMAN. Well...

JANE. I am Jane!

ALL. Jane!

JANE. Say it, Norman! Feel the power!
NORMAN. I am... really embarrassed.
JANE. I am Jane!
ALL. Jane!
NORMAN. Janey, look...
JANE *(grabbing him)*. Norman, at last count over thirty-seven thousand people in eighteen countries wanted to be me.
NORMAN. That's, uh, pretty impressive, Jane.
JANE. The power of me is electric, Norman. Take it. I have more than enough to share.
NORMAN. Oh, I get that sense. Yes.
JANE. Be me, Norman! Be me!
NORMAN. I am very close to being convinced.
JANE. Kneel, Norman! *(She pushes him to his knees. She takes her book and "dubs" him with it.)* Norman, by the power and authority of Jane, I hereby dub you my surrogate, and grant you all the privileges and feelings that come with that illustrious position. *(She drops the book and pulls him to her.)* Will you take it, Norman? Will you?
NORMAN. Yes! Yes! Oh, Jane, yes!

> *(She pushes him away; he lands in a heap on the floor, entirely dazed and spent. Jane crosses back to where she was and continues the narration. This time, Norman attacks the part with gusto, energetically acting out what Jane dictates.)*

JANE. It is night. Oh, the agony of my situation! I cry to the gods, "How could you? Oh, why have I been so cursed?" *(Every time Jane quotes herself, Norman mouths the words.)* I feel as if I am chained to my desk with the shackles of my responsibility. The paper!
ALL. The paper!
JANE. The paper!

ALL. The paper!

JANE. The ever-accursèd paper. A specter arises behind me - vile, insistent, breath reeking of coffee and chives, the bane of my existence - Mrs. Sniperly. "Mrs. Sniperly!" I cry to the specter, "why must we do this?" And she replies...

MRS. SNIPERLY *(formed by Mrs. Sniperly and Groupies 10-12)*. Well, Jane, why must anyone do anything? Growth requires challenges, and, as your teacher, my mandate is to encourage growth through challenges.

JANE. "No!" I scream. "Be gone, wretched specter!" But still, it speaks further.

MRS. SNIPERLY. When you have accomplished the writing of this paper, I feel that you will look back on the experience with satisfaction, knowing that you have tackled a tough task and overcome it.

JANE. And then she begins to torture me with The Dreaded and Awful Requirements.

MRS. SNIPERLY. The topic of the paper is The Moral Dilemma of Huckleberry Finn and Its Relationship to Current Day Situations. Length: 2500-3000 words. Your thesis should be found at the end of the first paragraph. All paragraphs should consist of at least seven complete sentences...

JANE. On and on the specter spouts her incessant list - requirement after requirement, stinging, slapping, jabbing, burning.

GROUPIE 10. Complete sentences, Jane.

GROUPIE 11. Back up your thesis.

GROUPIE 12. Appropriate diction.

GROUPIE 10. No spelling errors, Janey.

GROUPIE 11. Correct punctuation.

GROUPIE 12. Cite your page numbers, Jane.

JANE. "Be gone, foul spirits; for the love of all that is holy, leave me in peace!" I plead. But no. Instead, the specter speaks on:

MRS. SNIPERLY. Remember, Jane, the paper is the final major grade of both the marking period and the year. Given your marks thus far, you've placed quite a lot of pressure on this project. But you'll come through. It's due Friday morning, without fail. And Jane...

JANE. "Don't!" I plead. "Don't say it; not... the word." I hear it coming like a bullet train down the tracks, like a bowling ball down the lane. And I am tied to those tracks. And I am the number one pin! "Please don't say it!" But she does.

MRS. SNIPERLY. ... don't procrastinate.

ALL *(moving in to surround Norman as they chant)*. Procrastinate, procrastinate, procrastinate, procrastinate.

JANE. Nooooo!

MRS. SNIPERLY. Because if you procrastinate...

ALL. Procrastinate, procrastinate, procrastinate, procrastinate.

MRS. SNIPERLY. ... you may *(sudden change in the speech and the nature of the Sniperly Specter, becoming menacing)* fail the paper and the class and all chances of success will swirl into the sewer and you, Jane, will be finished!

JANE. "Save me!" I scream to whatever god might listen. "Oh, save me, save me!" The specter dissolves *(As Mrs. Sniperly fades away, all of the other Groupies return to their positions as fixtures in Jane's room.)* and I am thankful for that, but nothing can melt the icy realization that the paper still lies before me, not a word done, and the deadline looms a mere ten hours away. I sit in dazed silence, then reach for the on button of my computer. As I turn it on and it boots up, I hear and sense a sinister presence, far off but palpable, drawing ever nearer: Time.

TIME *(with others)*. Tick-tock, tick-tock, tick-tock, tick-tock.

JANE. I turn to the computer, ignoring the sound and the sense of impending time, using all of my will to focus on the words in front of me. I type.

COMPUTER. The Moral Dilemma of Huckleberry Finn and Its Relationship to Current Day Situations.

JANE *(over the sound of the computer)*. The words as they appear on the screen soothe my disquieted spirit for a moment. I feel ennobled by the work, hopeful that, yes, I will conquer after all.

COMPUTER. A Report by Jane.

JANE. I sit back and read what I have written, pleased. I have a title. If I can only persevere, I will soon have more words, and then more, and more, until I am finished. I hear singing, a celebration of my name, and I let it engulf me in a pleasing reverie.

NYMPHS OF SLUMBER *(as if singing a radio ad for soap, circa 1930)*. Janey, Janey, Janey, Jane,
Too much work makes you insane,
You should get some sleep right no-ow.

Janey, Janey, pretty one,
The moon is up and not the sun,
You should get some sleep right no-ow.
Do-do-do-do do-do-do...

JANE *(over the do-doing)*. The Nymphs of Slumber have come, surrounding me, wafting their pleasing sounds like the mild scent of vanilla. My eyes begin to close. I almost surrender to their wiles, but far, far away, I can still hear Time.

TIME *(and others)*. Tick-tick, tick-tick, tick-tick...

JANE. Time, marching ever closer. I awake suddenly, dispelling the Nymphs of Slumber. "Be gone,

Nymphs! I'll not cavort with you until my work here is done." I return to my computer, but something has happened. The words I had written before, about which I had felt vast accomplishment, now seem to mock me.

COMPUTER. The Moral Dilemma of Huckleberry Finn and Its Relationship to Current Day Situations. A Report by Jane.

(The room erupts in derisive laughter. Sections of the wall ridicule Norman-as-Jane as he runs around the room, looking for escape.)

WALL SECTION 1. A report? It's a stupid title, that's all!

WALL SECTION 2. Only twenty-five hundred more words to go, Janey!

WALL SECTION 3. What do you know about the moral dilemma of Huckleberry Finn? What do you care?

WALL SECTION 4. What are you going to write next, Janey, huh?

JANE. And Time creeps closer and closer. I can hear the demon whispering in my ear:

TIME. Nine hours, four minutes, twelve seconds left, Jane. Eleven seconds. Ten seconds. Tick-tock, tick-tock.

JANE. Think! I urge myself. You just need a beginning, some sort of angle... just one good idea. The ideas begin to come, but, one by one, they are killed.

GROUPIE 13. Okay, we could start like this: Huckleberry Finn is a character filled with conflict. The most important conflict that faces him is...

GROUPIE 14 *(very sarcastic)*. Oh, that's brilliant. That'll definitely work. Oh, yeah - that's just the way to go.

GROUPIE 15. How about this:
There once was a boy named Huck
His pap didn't...

GROUPIE 16. Censor that! Filth! Sickness! Thank you so much for your contribution to the downfall of American morals.

GROUPIE 17. How about beginning with a personal experience? Like, "When I was about Huck Finn's age, I had a dog named Bluebird."

(The Groupies raise their thumbs as if in favor of the idea, then suddenly turn their thumbs down and give it a big raspberry.)

GROUPIE 18. Here it is: If Huckleberry Finn were my friend, here is the advice I would give him. And then I make the whole paper into this letter to Huck, this real personal thing. *(Groupie 19 walks over to her as she speaks.)* What do you think? And at the end, I sign it, Your Good Friend, Jane. Huh? Huh? What do you say?

(Groupie 19 punches 18 in the stomach, then steps on her toe, then delivers a mighty blow to the chin, sending her flying back into her place in the wall. The rest of the Groupies add appropriate sound effects.)

JANE. Nothing occurs to me. The angels of inspiration have apparently folded their golden wings *(bird call sound effect)* and croaked *(loud belch)*. Then, I hear the voice I both despise and adore.

PROCRASTINATION *(a boy, very handsome)*. Hiya, Janey.

JANE. Procrastination!

PROCRASTINATION. You hungry, sweetheart?

JANE. "I... I am feeling a bit... famished, come to think of it," I say. My resolve is weakening in the face of my arch-friend, my beloved enemy, Procrastination.

PROCRASTINATION. I'll tell you what. Why don't we... ?

(Norman-as-Jane has been getting increasingly bothered by Procrastination's aggressive romantic advances. When Procrastination slips his arm around him, Norman can bear it no longer.)

NORMAN *(making a time out sign with his hands)*. Uh, Jane? Jane?

JANE. Norman, what are you doing?

NORMAN *(to Procrastination)*. Back away from me. Go lie down. Jane, I feel extremely privileged to be you, I want you to know that. But this... this is really not working well for me, this particular part. Could Procrastination be played by, you know, a girl?

(Jane looks to Procrastination, questioning.)

PROCRASTINATION. Wouldn't hurt my feelings. He's ugly.

JANE. Okay. But no more substitutions.

NORMAN. Oh, no. No, no. Just this one.

JANE *(to a Groupie)*. Cecelia, would you... ?

(Cecelia comes over and puts her arm around Norman, as Procrastination had been trying to earlier. She obviously has no problem with the role.)

NORMAN. Oh, this is a lot better. Thanks, Jane.

JANE. Can we go on?

NORMAN. As soon as possible, thank-you very much.

CECELIA. Why don't we just go down and get a little snack, hm? And then we could watch a television show. Just an hour's break. You deserve it.

NORMAN. Yes, I do.

JANE. Norman!

NORMAN. Oh, sorry.

JANE. "No," I say to Procrastination. "I have to finish this paper. I've been with you too much lately."

CECELIA. Too much? Jane, you've been in this room for forty-five minutes now, slaving away. That's unreasonable, baby, completely unreasonable. Come sit with me. We'll watch some television.

JANE. "No," I say, but my resolve is weakening.

CECELIA. How about a snack, then? Let's find some chocolate.

JANE. Oh, she knows how to get to me. "Choco, choco... no, no, I have to finish this. Please." And then the Nymphs return.

NYMPHS *(singing, same tune as previous)*. Janey, Janey, Sweet Baboo,
There's only so much you can do;
you have to get some sleep right now.

Janey, Janey, don't forget,
it's not attractive if you sweat;
you really should get sleep right now.
Do-do, do-do, do do do...

CECELIA *(coming in over the do-do's of the Nymphs)*. Jane, you're killing yourself here, for nothing. Time is on your side, Sweetheart; you'll be much more effective after a nap. Come on. Surrender. Surrender to the sweet embrace of sleep. It's not procrastination at all... it's incubation. You're giving your ideas a chance to hatch in the warmth of slumber.

JANE. I try to resist. Heaven knows I try, but those crooning voices rock me like a baby in a hammock made of clouds. "I really should do some more..." I try to say.

CECELIA. Sh, Janey. No more. Not now. Sleep, baby. Sleep. Sleep.

JANE. I collapse. The Nymphs of Slumber take me away to their soft, dark world of rest.

> *(The do-do's of the Nymphs fade awake. Cecelia softly says "sleep, sleep, sleep." The lights fade so everyone is in silhouette. Finally, for a long moment, there is no sound but the soft breathing of Norman-as-Jane.)*

JANE. I dream.

> *(The room flies apart, the Groupies twirling and moving to get to the next formation. As they move, they whisper and repeat previous lines, creating the sense of Jane moving into a dreaming state: "Have to get some sleep." "The paper, Janey, the paper." "2500 words, due tomorrow." "Don't procrastinate, Jane. Don't procrastinate." "Got to get it done." The Groupies create a mountain with Norman-as-Jane climbing it. Once the formation is set, the whispering stops and lights come up.)*

JANE. I find myself clinging to the steep face of a mountain, slowly climbing to the top. Handhold by handhold, foothold by foothold, I painfully progress to the summit somewhere above me. I reach an impasse - every time I try to pull myself up farther, the rock slips beneath my hand or my foot. I reach, and the stones slide away like a stack of papers knocked from my desk. I look down to see that the rock face has become sheer as glass below me. I am trapped. I open my mouth to shout for help - no sound comes. I begin to shake, my muscles trembling with exertion. Above me, shining like the Holy Grail, I see my last chance: a knob sticking out of the rock. It looks strangely like a paperweight I had as a child. If I can just reach it, if I can pull myself up once more, just once more after that, I'll be on top. I reach and touch the handhold. I stretch harder, and my finger curls around it, then my other fingers, finally my entire hand. I test it - it seems ready to take my weight. I pull, every molecule of my energy focused on that protrusion of stone under my hand. I am going to make it! I know, at last, I am going to make it! Up, up, up...

Suddenly, like the feet of a turtle snapping into its shell, everything supporting me disappears. *(The "mountain" of Groupies tumbles apart. Several Groupies catch Norman-as-Jane and flip him upside-down as he "plummets.")* I fall.

My mouth flies open, my arms stretch wide as I twist and spin through the void. Down I plunge, down, down, down. I sense only that when I stop plummeting, Death alone will catch me.

What is this? The air has grown thick, my descent has slowed. I right myself and float to solid ground. I have entered a slow motion world, as if, as if... as if I were under water. *(The Groupies have formed an underwater world - some make the sound of bubbles while imitating fish, turtles, waving coral, manta rays, etc.)* And I am. I am under a mile of ocean. Above me, the sun glows like an eye behind gauze. But how can I breathe? I think. My throat stops with fear. But I *am* breathing. I'm pulling air from the water as naturally as a fish.

Fish - they surround me! And a garden of shimmering coral waves to me, and manta rays brush my legs like cats, and the eels peek playfully from their caves. I swim amongst my new-found friends. I float and I fly in the breeze of the currents.

The fish talk to me. They open gaping mouths, saying what I think is four words over and over, but I cannot understand their burbled, bubbled syllables. I listen more closely; I am almost understanding. A sunfish is patiently trying to help me read its puckered lips. I shake my head. What? What is it?

I sense a presence behind me, feel its cold menace chilling my skin. I turn and face an enormous shark, and immediately I know its intention - to devour me. The fish's soft burbling transforms to wobbling screams as I turn and try to swim from the shark. I cannot move fast enough, and it catches my leg in its mouth. One leg, both legs, and higher it stuffs itself with my body. Incredibly, my mind realizes for a split second that I am caught in the circumstances of a children's rhyme - oh, fiddle, it's swallowed my middle! And still the fish scream at me even as I am being eaten alive and I become desperate to know, as the shark is chewing on my chest, what, what, what they are saying to me. The shark's jaws have closed on my neck, oh heck, and in the last moment of my existence the words of the fish finally become clear.

ALL. Where is your paper? Where is your paper?
JANE. "My paper!" I scream back at them in bubbles of my own. "I'm devoured by a shark and you want to know about my... !" The jaws take a final snap upward. Oh, dread! It's swallowed my... !

I wake up.

I am breathing heavily, sweating from the death I have just experienced in dream. In the dim light of the coming dawn, black night giving way to gray, I sit in silence, in the gloom of approaching doom. I know full well what the dream means, and I feel the shark of my failure circling and ready to feed. Time, with sickening tick, whispers words of triumph.

TIME. Tick-tick, tick-tick, 4:30 in the morning, Jane. Tick-tick, tick-tick, you lose. Tick-tick, tick-tick, no paper, baby, it's not done. Tick-tick, tick-tick, I won.

JANE. Time climbs on me like an octopus, sticks its tentacles to my skull. I feel myself smothered in its grasp. I quiver and sink and fall.

(Slowly, quietly, a beat begins from the crowd. Here and there we hear "Jane" spoken. The cadence increases in intensity.)

JANE *(cont)*. You think it's over, don't you, oh ye of little faith?
You think I stay beneath that pile, let Time have its dismal way?
Well, you've forgotten something: You must have forgotten my name.
Because in those letters - J-A-N-E - is the power behind my fame.
I'm Jane.
ALL. Jane!
JANE. "Enough!" I cry, "enough of this!" I clutch Time's awful throat.
With one quick squeeze I heave it away like a mangy, stinking goat.
The computer, still on, shudders and shakes, tries to shrink from my heated touch.
But I press those keys, grind out those words; in the end, it can't do much.
Just can't do much beneath the touch of one heated... undefeated... won't be cheated... shapely-seated... Jane!!

COMPUTER. In the novel *The Adventures of Huckleberry Finn*, by Mark Twain, also known as Samuel Langhorne Clemens, the moral dilemma faced by the main character, Huck, is a difficult one.

JANE *(over the sound of the computer)*. This I will admit: I had come close to failure. My first impulse upon awakening - my brain still haunted with the memory of those nightmares, my ears shattered by Time's relentless tick, my eyes speared by the meager words on the screen - my first impulse had been to curl up and wait for the specter to come for me, to hear its crackling voice:

SPECTER. No paper, Jane? No? Well, then, you have no choice but to FAIL... fail... fail... fail...

JANE. For a moment, I had been ready to lie down and die. But deep in my chest, buried in my heart, encased in armor of tempered steel, is a warrior. *(Thump-thump from the crowd)* Warrior Jane. *(Thump-thump)* Who can write a paper at 4:30 in the morning. *(Thump)* No problem-o. The words stream from my fingers like steam rolling from a pot, like butter dripping off an ear of corn, like chocolate melting on your tongue.

ALL. Mmmm.

COMPUTER. Furthermore, Huckleberry Finn's decision to stay with the Grangerfords might be said to mirror the current state of affairs in our educational system. That is to say that...

JANE. On and on I type, but not without obstacles. The Nymphs of Slumber hover around me, sighing and singing their luscious lullabies.

NYMPHS OF SLUMBER *(singing)*. Janey, Janey, you're so smart;
This paper is a work of art;
Why don't you take a nap right now?

JANE. "Away!" I say, "I'm done with you. Go and sing to someone else. I will not sleep until the twenty-five hundredth word is typed. Be gone!" And they are. Tentacled Time revives itself, tries to tick-tick in my ear. I slap it like the mosquito it is and say, "Get out of here." Words I become and sentences; paragraphs are my bones. At each new line I feel stronger, more sure the battle is mine. On page six, though, I hit a snag, a dam in my river of thought.

COMPUTER. While most of us realize the difference between right and wrong, Huckleberry Finn did not always have this advantage. He... he... his...

JANE. The sweet perfume of Procrastination wafts into my room. She senses my vulnerable moment, oozes on in, her moves as smooth as ever.

CECELIA. Hiya, Janey. Nice paper. You'll get it done, no sweat. Come take a little break.

JANE. For a moment, I swoon, her proposition just the trap I want to fall into. I stand, ready to leave my desk and go with her, when the next words of the paper occur to me. "Procrastination," I tell her, "I cannot go with you. Not now."

CECELIA. Janey, Sweet-ums, you know you want to.

JANE. "Be gone!" I cry.

(Norman can't stand the turn of events.)

NORMAN. Uh, Jane?

JANE. Norman, what are you doing? You're interrupting my rhythm. I'm carefully building to the climax.

NORMAN. I don't want to get in the way of that, Jane, but...

(He whispers in her ear.)

JANE. Norman! The Chronicles of Jane are a sacred document; the words of the text have been carefully crafted to reveal subtle characterizations, intense emotions, earth-moving plot structures. You are asking me to alter them purely to serve your selfish, salacious desires. You should be utterly ashamed of yourself!

NORMAN. Uh-huh. Will you do it?

JANE. I will not.

NORMAN. Awww, Janey...

JANE. Get back to your place.

NORMAN *(complying)*. Geez.

JANE *(back to the story)*. "Be gone!" I tell Procrastination, and with many backwards glances, she leaves. But before she goes, I call her back for one sweet kiss.

(Norman is surprised and delighted that Jane has given him his chance after all. He makes the best of the moment. At the end of the kiss, he turns and gives Jane a big thumbs up, mouthing the words, "Thank-you!")

JANE *(cont)*. At last, all foes vanquished, my final obstacle overcome, I press on with my paper. Specters, demons, nymphs, detractors, distracters, destroyers... all, all have fled, leaving me, Jane, the typing Queen. Page seven.

COMPUTER. While many may feel that Twain's writing has little relevance to our current political situation, indeed, such an assumption...

JANE. Page eight! *(The drumming begins, building slowly, as Jane gets closer and closer to finishing.)* The fingers fly, the thoughts unwind;
I'm a Mark Twain paper fool.

Some others may fold beneath this weight,
But I'm taking this thing to school.
Page Nine!

    COMPUTER. It must also be remembered that those who hold on to such prejudices inevitably suffer the consequences.

    JANE. Now, listen, y'all, I don't want to boast,
But I'm coming up on page number ten;
And like Johnny in that fiddle song,
I'm the best that's ever been.

    COMPUTER. Thus one can see that the moral dilemma of Huckleberry Finn does, in fact, have great relevance in today's society.

    JANE. The End *(thump)*. I am Jane *(thump, thump)*. I push the button to look at the word count; I close my eyes as it computes. I breathe deep. I look.

    COMPUTER. Two thousand five hundred and two words. 7:15 a.m. Score: Time: 0, Jane: 1. End of game. Jane wins.

    JANE. Yes, yes, yes, yes, yes... *(She gets the Groupies worked into a frenzy of dancing and jumping, Norman happiest of all.)* I'm Jane!
    ALL. Jane!
    JANE. Don't forget my name!
    ALL. Name!
    JANE. I've got the brain!
    ALL. Brain!
    JANE. No more of this pain!
    ALL. Pain!
    JANE. I broke the chain!
    ALL. Chain!
    JANE. 'Cause I am Jane!
    ALL. Ja...

(Someone screams; everyone shrinks from a figure who enters from the left. As Jane speaks the next lines, the Groupies go back to their places as the room.)

JANE. I have celebrated too soon. The struggle I thought I had won suddenly grows a new face, a sneering face, a face that covers a skull, a skull that cradles a brain, a brain with a single desire: to make me suffer. Into my room has slithered my brother, the evil Stewart. Part of me panics.

GROUPIE 20. It's too much! It's just too much! We've fought the... and the nymphs, we... we can't take anymore! Stop the madness. Someone stop the madness!

JANE. I quickly quell that quivering part of me. *(Two Groupies quickly grab Groupie 20, dragging her back into the wall.)* I can't afford a moment's loss of focus. Not now, not with Stewart in the room, standing so close to the possibility of my demise.

STEWART. Hello, Janey-Painey.

JANE. "Hello, Stewart," I say, trying to keep my eyes locked on his, not wanting to let him realize that there, only three feet from his foot, is the plug-in for my computer. And I have not saved the paper.

GROUPIE R. I told you I'd be important, didn't I? Huh? See? See? I told you!

STEWART. What are you working on, Janey?

JANE. Why do you ask, Stewart?

STEWART. Well, I was just curious, Jane-Pain-Lame-Brain, why I had to get woken up at 4:30 this morning by you tap-tap-tap-tapping on your keyboard.

JANE. The Stewart beast is always surly, but when it doesn't get its full ration of sleep, it is nasty to the nth degree.

STEWART. Must be a pretty important project to get you up that early, huh, Janey?

JANE. He bends down and reaches toward the power plug, and I know he knows, and he knows I know he knows. I breathe deeply, try to stay nonchalant. "No," I say, "it's not that important."

STEWART. So you wouldn't mind if I just yanked this plug then?

JANE. I flinch. As hard as I try, I can't help it. Stewart grins like a gargoyle, and a hundred murderous thoughts pop into my head.

GROUPIE 21. Throw him out the window, Jane.

GROUPIE 22. Boil him in oil.

GROUPIE 23. Ax him.

GROUPIE 24. Shoot him.

GROUPIE 25. Take his puny little head and twist it and twist it until it pops off and then put it on a stake and parade around the town... *(She looks around, realizes she has gone overboard.)* Get him, Jane.

JANE. "Stewart, leave the plug alone," I tell him.

STEWART. What's it worth?

JANE. I don't negotiate with terrorists, you little...

STEWART. Get back! Get back or I'll pull this plug, Jane; you know I will.

JANE. Well do I know his threat is not idle. Just as I had superglued his head to the pillow the week before, and just as he had fed thumbtacks to my gerbil the week before that, he would pull that plug.

STEWART. Give me a dollar figure, here, Jane... I'm listening. Cash. Small bills only. Unless you've got big ones. Because I'll take those.

JANE. He is stupid, but no less dangerous because of it. I begin a long threat, calculated to give me time to think.

STEWART. What are you going to give me, Janey? Huh?

JANE. Stewart, let me put it this way: if you pull that plug, you'll pay for the rest of your life. You'll still be paying in your afterlife.

STEWART. Fifty bucks, Jane.

JANE. Generations from now, you great-great-great-great granddaughter will feel the pain resulting from this action. And so will her dog. If you pull that plug, your punishment will be so severe that the fleas on that dog will suffer. Are you understanding me?

STEWART. Forty bucks, Jane-Brain-Pain, and that's my final offer.

JANE. I keep talking, and all the while I talk, I plan. My mind isn't on the words I am speaking to him, but on the space between me and that evil being. Inch by inch, I move closer to him. Finally, I am in position. In my mind's eye, I have seen what I will do. I need but one thing more: a distraction. I haven't time to contrive anything elaborate; fortunately, The Evil Stewart's minuscule intelligence allows me to employ simple means. Still, timing is crucial. I wait until he is in full yap before unleashing my tactic.

STEWART. Gee, Janie, my fingers just seem to be aching to pull this plug. Unless I get some money very soon, I don't think I can control them. Here they go, Janie, here...

JANE. I strike. "Ma, Stewart's bugging me," I lie. My intense concentration slows time. In the half of a half of a second that Stewart takes to look back, ready to claim, "I'm not doing nothing, Ma!", I take one step toward him. His hand has left the power cord. I must make contact before he touches it again. As the Evil Stewart turns back to face me, realizing he has been duped, I launch into the air. I see the terror in his face; I have become a missile, fully armed with destructive intent and fingernails. As I come to the apex of my arch in the air, I see the choice he is making - reach for the cord or brace for attack? He braces. I prepare for impact. Hands, knees, fingers, elbows, feet - all transform from mere appendages to severe instruments of punishment. The first fist lands on the side of his head, the second connects with his ribs. As I fall on him, my knee rams into his thigh, rendering one mighty charlie horse. I need do little more. The Evil Stewart becomes an armadillo, a road-killed specimen at that. I yank him up by his ear and send him out the door with a kick to the backside.

I turn. My heart slams beneath my ribs. Victory wants to shout, begins to whisper my name.

GROUPIES. Jane, Jane, Jane, Jane...

JANE. I stifle it. I will not rejoice too early again. When the paper rests in my hand, then, perhaps, will I shout. Not before. Things can still go awry. I walk to the computer. I press a button.

COMPUTER. Print?

JANE. Yes.

COMPUTER. The whole thing?

JANE. Yes. I wait, ready for the next battle. Lightning could still strike. A virus could still infect. A meteorite could still crash through the roof. The printer could still jam.

GROUPIE 26. What's taking it so long??

JANE. At last, page one emerges, clean and crisp. And then page two. And three. With each page, the knot in my chest frays and unravels. Six, seven, eight... two pages to freedom. Two pages. Nine comes forth. Then, almost reluctantly, page ten slides onto the pile in all its word-covered glory. Truly, this time, I am done. *(The group lets out a large sigh of relief. Jane crosses back to the over-sized book, puts the small book on the shelf, and closes the door.)* Thus endeth the Chronicle of Jane, Book Seven - The Term Paper. Amen.

    ALL *(like monks)*. Amen.

    JANE *(coming out into the audience, lit by a follow spot)*.
Now, before we go, there's one last thing,
A fact well worthy of mention:
It's the sort of detail you might have missed
If you've not paid complete attention.

Throughout this story I'm sure you saw
That my fight with my foes was terrible.
It would be quite natural for you to wonder
How I overcame odds so unbearable.

The very next thought I think might sprout
Is about *you* putting on this show.
Given the same set of circumstances,
Would you rise up from below?

The answer to that, I'm here to say,
Is a resounding and definite... no.

Don't get me wrong; you've got your talents,
Those traits that some come to see,
But in cases extreme like you've just seen,
Trouble is, you're just not me.

Because...

I'm Jane.

    (Jane runs off as the lights come up brightly on stage to reveal the cast in formation, ready to perform the final percussion/dance sequence. They drum, dance, jump, cartwheel, leap, and in

every other way exhibit all of the physical energy that characterizes teenagers. Norman has slipped off his dress during Jane's previous speech; he becomes part of the rest of the Groupies.)

ALL *(thunderous).* Jane!

(At one point, the Groupies slow down; the rhythm calms. Four "Jazz Groupies" perform.)

JAZZ GROUPIE 1. You know Janey?
JAZZ GROUPIE 2. She wrote the paper.
JAZZ GROUPIE 3. She did?

(The above three lines are repeated over and over as Jazz Groupie 4 performs. A fifth Groupie performs with Jazz Groupie 4, improvising a drum solo on his body.)

JAZZ GROUPIE 4. That Janie. She can do anything. That Janie - she's a marvel. Jane. Whoa. Name it. Go on, name it. I dare you to name it. Name the one thing that Janey, Janey, Janey, Jane can't do. Go on. Go on! Go on, go on, go on, go on, go on, name it! You can't. You just can't. Because... *(pause for drum solo)* because... *(more solo)*... because *(more solo, building to a climax. When Jazz Groupie 4 begins to repeat "cause, cause, cause" in quick succession, everyone moves into three circles - one small center circle, a second larger one formed around it, and the third largest around the center two. Jane sneaks onstage to crouch in the middle of the center circle.)*

JAZZ GROUPIE 4, JOINED BY ALL. 'Cause, 'cause, 'cause, 'cause... *(This word is repeated until the circles are formed. Then, the circles begin to spin, the center one clock-wise, the next out counter-clockwise, the outer ring clock-wise. As they spin, the Groupies yell:)* Sheeeeeeeeeeeeeeeeeee's... Jane!

(All of the Groupies fall to the floor as Jane suddenly reveals herself from the center circle.)

JANE. You just can't do much without the touch of one heated, won't-be-cheated, shapely seated, undefeated... JANE!!!

* * *

OTHER TITLES AVAILABLE FROM BAKER'S PLAYS

EYES WIDE OPEN

Jennifer Kirkeby

Drama, High Schools / 2m, 5f

Eyes Wide Open is a touching and informative play about Kristin, a 16 year-old girl who suffers from anorexia and bulimia. Written by a woman who has experienced eating disorders first hand, the story begins after Kristin faints in her dance class. Kristin finds herself in a hospital room where she is met by the spirit of her grandmother, Birdy.

Birdy, who is seen only by Kristin, gently guides her granddaughter through moments of her life. As they revisit the dance studio, Kristin relives both joyful and unhappy experiences with her best friend, Amber. Michael, the boy who Kristin has a crush on, helps her to learn the dance steps. We meet Julia, an obnoxious student who loves to show her "creative" dances and give others fashion advice. Kristin helps Daniel, Michael's younger brother to stop his bad (and dangerous) habit of closing his eyes when he dances. Laura is the dance teacher who tries unsuccessfully to talk to Kristin about her eating disorder. Ultimately, these experiences and Birdy's guidance help Kristin to examine her life and make her final decision whether to live or die.

BAKERSPLAYS.COM

OTHER TITLES AVAILABLE FROM BAKER'S PLAYS

COPIES

Brad Slaight

Dramatic Comedy, Jr. High/High Schools / 2m, 6f

An an orientation camp for new teenage clones, teens are sent to "Camp I.M.U" fresh from the lab to make a transition into the world of the "Originals" who have ordered them made. The newest "Copy" (a word they prefer to "clone") to arrive is a very bright and positive teenager named Michael who soon realizes what the other copies in his cottage have known for awhile – that their stay at the camp is much longer than they had thought. Michael befriends a rebellious Copy named Melissa, who does not get along with her Original and refuses to change her attitude in order to please her. She informs Michael, and the other Copies, that she is going to escape from the camp and fight for what she calls "copy rights". This is a story right out of tomorrow's headlines. Not good at math? Have a clone of yourself made from your own DNA, but gifted in math to do your problems for you. Need a spare part for the future? Your clone is a walking talking parts store. *Copies* explores the heart and soul of clones, bred specifically to do all those things you don't want to do

BAKERSPLAYS.COM

OTHER TITLES AVAILABLE FROM BAKER'S PLAYS

STAGE KISS

Michael R. Kramer

*Comedy, High School/Community Theatre /
1m, 2f / Simple set*

Kevin and Jill meet during auditions for a community theatre play. Kevin immediately expresses his dismay about the director's decision to have the actors read a kiss scene, with real kissing required. What starts as a debate between two strangers about the wisdom of the director's demands evolves into a funny and fragile connection as two lonely individuals confront their insecurities about romance, sex, and, of course, kissing.

*"A story about a cute, romantic tryst"
- City Edition, Milwaukee*

BAKERSPLAYS.COM

OTHER TITLES AVAILABLE FROM BAKER'S PLAYS

CANDIDA

George Bernard Shaw
Adapted and Abridged by Aurand Harris

Comedy / 3m, 2f / Interior

Probably Shaw's most popular play, *Candida* recounts the love sickness of young poet Eugene Marchbanks for Candida, wife of the Rev. Morell. At first, Morell is amused; but when he begins to doubt his wife's love, he becomes disturbed and angered. The poet becomes the stronger suitor, Morell realizes his weaknesses and Candida, one of the most remarkable women in dramatic literature, gives strength to her husband and teaches Marchbanks how to love. Harris offers a superb adaptation for competition, for study, and for introduction to one of the classics of modern theatre.

BAKERSPLAYS.COM

OTHER TITLES AVAILABLE FROM BAKER'S PLAYS

TARTUFFE

Adapted from Moliere by Charles Jeffries
and Luis Muñoz

Comedy / 8m, 7f

So virtuous is Tartuffe that every form of pleasure is an abomination to him. Orgon, a rich merchant, is completely duped by the ruse and watches approvingly as the cunning Tartuffe "reforms" his whole family. So besotted is the merchant that he even plans to give Tartuffe his fortune, his house, and finally his daughter! Orgon's wife finally exposes Tartuffe for the rogue he is – and her husband for being a gullible fool. By the time Orgon sees the light, only the courts can insure justice. This clever adaptation of the Moliere classic calls for an energetic ensemble. Moliere's greatest work is expertly adapted for one-act competition by the authors of *The Beggar's Opera*, *The Merry Wives of Winsor*, and *Valpone*.

BAKERSPLAYS.COM

www.ingramcontent.com/pod-product-compliance
Lightning Source LLC
Chambersburg PA
CBHW072339300426
44109CB00042B/1951